First Drafts from the Brewery

Rowe Carenen

Attention schools and businesses: for discounted copies on large orders, please contact the publisher directly.

For information contact:

Unsolicited Press

Portland, Oregon

www.unsolicitedpress.com

orders@unsolicitedpress.com

619-354-8005

Cover Design: Kathryn Gerhardt

Editor: Kristen Marckmann

ISBN: 978-1-956692-12-9

For James,
for reasons

Table of Contents

First Drafts from the Brewery

I ate a fig

from a tree I do not
own. Yet.

It was almost sweet —
juice dripping from the
pulp, tickling past lips
tart on my tongue.

I want to see
what else can grow

in this fertile place
within the chained fence.

There will be books
stacked and shelved
in every room.

I will shine light
in the caves, turn
the mud walls into

a gallery of past pleasures
and present plans.

I'm sorry, thank you (a note to my body)

I'm sorry—
>
> it took me so long to feed you
> that you stopped believing you
> deserved to be fed;

that I've pinched
>
> you beyond the place of reason
> to fit into a fantasy;

for not listening when you whispered
>
> you needed rest or a Mounds bar;

you were not loved and lingered over,
>
> and I believed when he said
> such awful things about you;

I didn't see that neglect and obsession
>
> destroyed the tenuous
> balance of your spirit's home.

Thank you—
>
> for sturdy legs carrying me miles more
> than the marathon and beyond
> every finish line;

for repairing yourself after every blasted
surgery and helping me survive
menopause so I could teach Mom;

for mirroring the deep cheekbones
        of the women who came before me;

for strong arms that comfort puppies
        and kittens, grownups and babies,
        and me;

for teaching me that forgiveness
        is housed in every curve
        and angle;

because you get up
        every morning
and move me.

Car Talk with Christine

After seven hours on our feet
seeing to every detail—
perfectly tied bows, his Bud
Light and her Chardonnay, only
biodegradable confetti thrown
and washed away from
the Huguenot Loft steps—
of strangers' happily ever
after, we sit in her station
wagon and talk of the end
of mine.

She apologizes, and I don't
understand why. "I should've
known." "I didn't tell you."
"But I should've been there."
"You were."

I remind her that she promised
her home would always
be my safe house, her daughter
my heart, her love my mirror
to see the self I feared I lost.

Kintsugi

The Japanese don't believe in broken
beyond repair. That's what gold
is for. Fill the cracks, seal pieces,
marry the old with new.

Bone teacups knit by filament,
dust, and resin, more beautiful
for the near-shattering fall.

Are the fragments of my heart
large enough to be held
together by metal or
will new shards
be cauterized
to my breastbone?

Should you see the aortic
powder, please grab
the dustpan and sweep.

The slivers of my splintered self
may need more than gold.

Sanctuary

It is Sunday, pre-noon,
and I've missed church. Again
I was texting with the surveyor
who will mark my land
before the fence guy comes Tuesday
to begin work on the paid-for privacy.

I let the breeze dry my frizz, sip
something burnt and lovely
in a gifted mug while I read
an advanced copy of Leesa Cross-Smith's
So We Can Glow.

Her first story, "We, Moons," has me
sighing and agreeing and my heart
can't decide if we are jealous or proud
of our unmet best friend who
stitches truth with a thread
made of all the words
we both know. I settle
on pride and jot her a note,
effusive, adoring. And grateful.
I am fed full by this honest
woman who tells truth tales
and feels familiar as a thumb-
holed hoodie. I want everyone
to read everything she writes; I take
pictures and send them to friends,
"Look! This is genius. This, right here,
is the why."

Southern Comfort

I do not know how to help
when his eyes grow wide
locked on mine until he worries
that loss will spill down, drip
off his beard, splash his collar.

I do not know what to tell him
when he asks me the whys
that I'll never be able to answer
because I won't ever know
what caused those men to be stolen
away from families who could never
prepare for the emptiness that moves in
to closets, breakfast nooks, a burgundy F150.

I do not know how to comfort someone
who has spent days, weeks, a lifetime,
squaring his shoulders, and cutting
into his collarbone to store his grief,
making room.

I am not accustomed
to the largess of his pain,
and I have no balm for the wounds.
So I pour another whiskey, sit,
and listen to bygone stories.

On Meeting Minerva Jane

"She was just so sad," I explained
to Evelyn when I came home an hour
later than intended from PetSmart.

I went in for a bulb for the turtle
that does not belong to me and spent
forty-seven minutes sitting on cold
concrete talking to the grey floof
who cowered in the corner
of her steel cage.

I told her how beautiful she was
and how anyone who picked a kitten
over her was stupid and knew nothing
about character and personality.
She kept eye contact
while I reminisced over Sylvia
who died just over a year ago.

Dinner was waiting and I had
to go, but I'd be back.

Every day for a week
I sat on that slab, asked
about her day, relayed my own

trials over tax law and audits
and name changes.
I'd sigh, she'd blink.

She once, on Thursday, came
to the edge and let me rub
her nose with my index finger.

Saturday, she rode home
in the too-expensive paisley
cat-carrier and promptly
disappeared under my bed.

Four months, and hours of conversation,
later, she jumped up, on her own,
sniffed my tea, and hurled her tiny body
into my side while I read of heroes
and quests for some long-forgotten somethings.

Now she talks to me
every day and I maintain eye-contact,
scratch her butt, and tell her
I'm glad she's not sad anymore.

A poem in parenthesis

I'm fine
(after crying in the car
for twenty minutes so hard
that I worry my contacts
will wash out and I won't
be able to drive home).

I understand
(that the one thing
keeping me from losing
my ever-loving mind
has been postponed,
again, and I should learn
to stop hoping so much).

I'm here
(for whatever he needs,
and I will carry his burden
and read his truth and volley
tumor humor back and try
to forget that my friend is dying,
and she doesn't even know
her husband and I are preparing
for the after).

I can do it
(whatever needs doing
to keep someone from drowning
because I learned to swim

before I learned to drive
and these waters haven't
claimed me yet).

I'm just tired
(so way deep beyond my bones
and blood that I don't believe
sleep will cure it,
and I can't track which
emotions are mine and I'm
not sure it matters
anymore).

Ginger love

While picking my bounced
darts off the brewery floor,
he asked me what I thought
would happen to her hair.

When tiny, a copper penny
kissed her head;
and summer made
blonde strawberries dance.

Now, it has deepened
and the brunette of generations
is staking claim, pushing
the aberration out.

But she is magic.

I believe the baby
rebel will do as she
pleases, from her toddler
toes to the tips
of the bows.

The imp's deviation shows
when the sun shines red
and he'll love her more.

Granddaddy's bookshelves

are broken down
again. The wooden screws
stripped to bare rivets,
and I remove the duct tape
holding the square peg
in place.

Some of the slats cracked
decades back
but the wood holds strong.

He made these for me
before they even held
Narnia and Wild Things.

Lemon Pledge then
Old English keeps
the shine across
two time zones,
five states,
thirteen, fourteen homes.

Rough hands carved
a tangible tenderness
the gruff old man
could never speak.

The first time

... I kissed your cheek
I lingered just above your beard
longer than I should've
and you tilted your head
to mine, just breathing, and I nearly
forgot to take off my seatbelt
when I tried to get out of your car.

... you held my hand
you were not tentative, certain
there was nothing I wanted more
than to be palm to palm with you,
holding almost tightly, our lifelines
melting into each other and the grooves
of conversation didn't even skip.

"So this is what we do now?"
"I guess so." "Good. I like it."

... I held your arm
I needed steadying, tired and my heels
high, so you took my hand through
the crook, resting my fingertips on your
forearm and I was shored up, stabilized
by the warmth of your skin pressed into mine
and the peek of your side smile.

... you kissed my mouth
you took my bottom lip between yours

and let your tongue dance beyond my teeth,
tasting hope realized and hunger whetted.
There were no awkward clinks and clashes,
only a homecoming, your self
meeting mine, steaming the windows.

Morning Commute

The best mornings begin
with extra cat-cuddles
enveloped in fresh sheets.

Out come the workout clothes—
leggings, sports bra, tank
(no socks, no shoes)—hair
pulled up and back and I head
to the spare room to punch
the lights out of an invisible assailant
or find some zen on the peacock
feather yoga mat.

And then it is time for tea.
So I set the kettle on, pick from
a plethora of mugs and even more
bags, boxes, loose leaf. The whistle
escapes from the navy lip,
the aroma aerates my home,
makes me smile. Always.

I take the steaming mug
and the heavy whipping cream
(added only after the tea is fully steeped)
to the meditation room where
I grab a devotional, palo santo,
and a stone or two for focus.
I sit cross-legged, balancing
all of the accoutrements,

and pull the quilt over my lap
making a nest for the grey lady
whose purrs become the soundtrack
for deep breaths and prayers.

The smoking stick, like incense, fills
the small space marking the time
as holy. I close my eyes, one hand
on the drooling cat, one holding a stone
to remind myself that anger isn't always
righteous, and breathe deep.

The timer dings in a blink
and Minerva flinches. I pour
a dollop of cream in the waiting cup,
open the book and read wisdom
generations old. I savor each sip
and set my mind for the day.

Sister-friends

These women come alongside me, wrapping
their arms around my waist, urging me along, kneeling
when my knees give out and the carpet burns bleed.

One would not let me live in the dark, came and found me
huddled in the couch corner. Ordered "Put on your bra we're
going out." But still held my hand, under the table, when I couldn't
answer polite queries about my day and the tears in my sweater.

Another drove up north to go antiquing, which I hate, to distract
from that which I still loved, drank my too-strong too-sweet pink
cocktail, watched a terrible movie just because the book was good,
when the time came moved me back home,
and left Earl Grey macarons in my mailbox.

One insisted I join in family dinners even when I wanted to hide
in an Ole Miss sweatshirt and ratty too-big jeans. Lent her husband
to move out the trash my husband left behind in the middle of my
living room. Let me sit with her babies who played Hot Lava Hot
Lava, watched movies, and made me jewelry on Valentine's Day so
I wouldn't be sad.

And another sent her mother and sister to take me to dinner and
tell me the truth about "Rowe-colored glasses." In her home there is
a room named for me by her daughter who crawls into my bed with
every visit.

I am shorn up by such love,
my heart groans at the growth.

Nana loved Cecilia,

humming the chorus as she
rinsed out the green pebbled
plastic juice cups, the names
of each grandchild printed in black
sharpie on the bottom.

It came on the radio once
when we were making sandwiches
in the boat's cabin. She turned
the volume up to seven, laughed,
and fussed at my stingy spread
of peanut butter with the pickle
on thick wheat bread.

Nine years later, two strokes, and one breast,
she sits at the breakfast nook, the locks
of her wheelchair secured, and I go
over the list of exercises designed
to keep her muscles from atrophying.
"Cecilia, you're breaking my heart..."
in her eye there's a grin
peeking through the grimace.

Morning Coverup

 You make me nervous, still,
Years, lifetimes later,
and I blush when you say
nice things or let me ramble
on about a novel/recipe/movie.
This, all of this, is a contradiction
because sometimes I can't keep
my head from spinning into
the what-ifs of it all blowing
up and feeling like napalm
would be a kindness.

It is not your fault
the ghosts haunt my
heart and whisper past
truths: I am a convenience,
a fallback, too much, not
enough, I don't fit.

You were not the one who
squished and patted my four-
time menopause pooch, suggesting
my two-a-days might not
be cutting it. It wasn't you
who noted I was "more" than any
girl you'd allowed to slide
naked into pilled sheets. You did
not say, "Now we're getting
somewhere" when the disease

stripped the softness
from my ribs/hips/face. The echoing
"you are just too hard to love,
I need someone easier," is not
your voice.

You are the one who
showed up to paint two
houses in less than ten
years and sneaks in to vacuum
and leave lilies in a sunshine
vase in the bedroom
because I'm up before
colors kiss the sky.
You followed in the Jeep
when I drove the folks
to the ER because Dad
couldn't do words or
remember my name.
You wrap me in your
safety, not letting loose
until you feel my tension
slip through the knots and I
finally relax into you.

It has taken a life cultivated
to be so full of me and a reminder
that I earned my soft swagger
because I grew this confidence
myself, and while I love every
dip and curve, I am unused
to someone else loving, too.

So forgive me if sometimes
I leave a tank on in the mornings.

Angel's Envy

A caramel cream
clings to the side of
swirling glass
and I sigh. I may
have fallen in love.

That first sniff tingles
and I hold my breath,
my nose the outlier
to carry the decadence.

A sip held on the back
of my tongue swims to
the front and my mouth
feels too small.

I want to see if oak
and vanilla will dance
away the buds, afraid
for just a moment that
I was wrong, that I
misremembered. But
I'm not. I didn't.

The swallow warms me
to my elbows, to my knees,
and the burn on my lips
can only be quenched by
one more taste.

Little Baby Sunshine Head is Eighteen and Off to College

When her mother told
me she was pregnant, I claimed
the baby as my own. Before she was
born, I mailed *The Very Hungry
Caterpillar* down to Florida
because I didn't know yet
onesies were more practical.

Finally meeting her, I couldn't
believe how her eyes, wide and round
like teacups, took in everything
around her. Her smile was fast,
shy, sure of her world, less sure
of me.

When she was three, her mother
made me lunch after an interview.
We sat at a picnic table, eating
sandwiches and grapes.
We lamented big girl woes while
little baby sunshine head smooshed
ham and cheese into the Weeble Wobble
mailbox because the postman might
need a snack.

When she was eleven,
she helped carve my first pumpkin
on the roof of the apartment.

She traced a cat, to honor Sylvia downstairs,
and did not judge my unsteady hand. Then
it was Christmas and I needed a tree, so she
and her mom tied the Douglas Fir to the roof
of the Scion and dragged it through the hallways
into the elevator, decorated with old
ornaments, new memories. She'd sometimes
stay the night after I walked over and picked her
up from school. We would order in Jimmy John's
with extra pickles, watch movies, and even
braid her hair. Once we got snowed in
and she downloaded a game on the iPad
for the cat to play while we cuddled in my too large bed.

Sixteen and her mother and Molly
drove her down for her first college visit.
She brought me a portrait of Minerva, the grey lady-
cat, that captured her sass so exactly I cried. Her mother
tried on wedding dresses and we ate bougie burgers and I
tried not to call her "kiddo."

Seventeen, she walked her mother down
the aisle and my heart hurt. She trained her cats, wrote
protests on signs, her shoes, built her own loom,
made tea, and cuddled her mom.

And now, she's getting ready to go away
to college and blow the universe
up with kindness. I know, I know, I know,

she's a whole grown-ass woman now, but
I can't let go of little girl who leaned over
during *Zootopia* and whispered, "this is about
racism, isn't it?" and sighed.

The kitten bites at the moon—

stone and silver bird nesting
between my breasts, purring
even more loudly when I thump
his nose to get him to quit.
The quiet is strange, no Elvis
or Milli Vanilli or mariachi
vibrating from the trailer
across the street. Even the felon
and his mother have not
begun shouting. Yet. I watch
leaves drop into the above
ground pool next to the church
with the not quite clever signs.
I want it to feel like fall
as I swing in my pumpkin
chair swallowing mouthfuls
of cardamon tea.
But it is nearly 80 in October
and I'm a bit bitter about it,
so I blast the AC when I go
inside and light the firewood candle.

I do not kiss your mouth,

only your cheek, twice.

You groan, barely, and
lean in, palm pressing
more firmly the slope below
the small of my back.

My fingers dig in
to shoulders broad
enough to carry burdens
that do not belong
to you.

I hold on when you bury
your scruff where my neck
meets my collarbone.

For just a minute
you pull back,
your lips lingering
on my jaw.

I sigh.

For My Favorite Cousin (don't tell the others)

So when she asked
us to read the prayer
at her Catholic wedding,
a thank you, I thought,
for reading scripture in mine,
I cried.

I remembered my shower—
she drove up from Florida,
that blasted state, in June
on her birthday, to celebrate
and I took her shopping.

We bought an entire
makeup counter and a whole
wall at Gap. She was beautiful
and I was proud.

I surprised her with a birthday
cake at my party, a silly
Mad Hatter all sliding
teals and pinks.

Later, after I'd left
my husband, fled
the state, and rested
in fear and shame,

she asked if I'd
drive up to Raleigh
to have dinner with her
and her still-new husband,
I hesitated.

But I went, blurting out
immediately after her
tight hug, "I know you
think I'm wrong, but..."

So when she asked
if I would be godmother
to her perfect, and sure
to be brilliant and beautiful,
Bean, I cried.
My shoulders drop tension

as I come in the back, and the breath
I didn't know I was holding
releases.

There are only good things
in my house. I fill it
with comfort and cuddles,
music and musings.

There is always beer
in the fridge, a glass frosting
in the freezer. Wine sits on the counter
above the cabinet with the rolling pin.

Thieves steals away
the smoked salmon smell
and Frankincense wafts
from the living room.

The walls—a gallery of stories
of decades and adventures past
(a canal map, a book, a turning tree)
whispers of those to come.

Disappearing Act

I think the last time
you went away hurt less.
It was cleaner.
There were so few
overlaps that when you
entered the ether, I just
missed you like a dream
that takes a few minutes
to shake when the covers
still feel like home.

But now you are a phantom
limb. Your absence is an ache
that is beyond the marrow,
present in every picture,
strumming the guitar
in every song.

I'm learning to remove
the we and us of it all,
get comfortable with singularity
and sharing the good with
just me.

Just me. I loved her well
not so long ago.

I'd forgotten, never had,
partnership and how rich
that cake.

Some people fall in love fast,

sprinters knowing that the finish
line is the beginning of the life
they've been running towards.

Some people fall in love fast
over a smirk, a side-eye,
a shared love of stinky cheese
for breakfast.

I have a friend who fell in love
with his wife's laugh—free,
unbound, no room for anything
but joy.

Others fall in love slow,
marathoners knowing each
footfall brings them to the Reynolds
wrap blankets of earned comfort.

Others fall in love slow
over decades of coffee and tea,
symphonies of pain and promise,
knowing the heart-song.

Hyena

He hated my laugh,
too loud, too hearty,
and I embarrassed him.

So I stopped.
For years.

I covered my mouth
and stomped out joy
so as not to make
him uncomfortable.

Even after I left,
and he remarried,
I muffled.

Few giggles,
no guffaws.

Because I was afraid
to cause shame.

But now? Now I throw
my head back
and I do not care
if I draw attention.

My happiness is mine
and no one owns it
but me.

Rest Stop

My sternum constricts
around the hollow space
where once was a pulsing passion
and the root of giggles.

I am tired
and have misplaced rest
somewhere among deadlines, house
chores, and receptions I'd rather skip.

Today I closed my office
door and cried, as quietly as I could,
careful to keep my makeup free
of streaks.

I turn my back on my monitor
and stare through the stripes
to the outside and pray
for wisdom, grace, kindness.

I'm ready for you to come
home and fold me into your
chest while my hands clutch
each other, pressing into
my heart.

Later I will stretch
my full-length across
your couch, resting my head

in your lap. Your fingers,
tough and tobacco-stained, will
get tangled in my curls and I'll
read you excerpts from some novel.

For now, it is enough
to know that in a week
I'll let myself in with my Hello Kitty
key, trudge up the warped
wooden stairs, say hi to the turtle,
drop my bag on the floor, and find rest.

Tearing Up

I realized last night sipping
mulled wine from Nana's mug
(she didn't like wine, but I think
she'd approve of this bottle from
Aldi, maybe even approve of you),
that you didn't actually break my heart.

The relief warmed me
beyond my sternum into places
I didn't know I was cold
(and you know part of me
is always cold and there are
never enough fuzzy socks
or book quilts to keep
the chills at bay).

Instead of breaking or even
bending this pump that picks
up speed at your name
your real laugh, you've only
torn it. Not ripped (from headlines,
sheets, comfort), but torn—
maybe along the perforation?

I'm not sure and now I'm delving
into semantics. But what I know is this:
you did it because I let you.

So here we are months/years/moments
later and I'm bleeding you
into my tea and to-do lists
that are so separate from you
that it feels almost like colonization.

What I need (golly what a statement
THAT is) is to figure out
if you get to come back
with needle apologies and
thread explanations
to stich back the ventricles

or

do I grab the stapler and do it
my own damn self.

Memorial Day 2019

It is too hot
as I sit on my porch
in my pumpkin chair.
The breeze tickles my toes
and makes the leaves
of the big oak tree sing.
I sip tea despite the heat
and it warms more than my chest.
Children are squealing, splashing
in the above ground pool
across the street and two doors down.
A souped-up Chevy, wheels taller than my Prius,
blasts "Gangsta's Paradise."
I've discarded the Czech novel
to read instead the shadows on my lawn.

Out Back of the Brewery

I almost feel sorry for Levi
who saunters over, squints,
tries not to spill APA
on torn jeans and Ramones shirt.
He plops down one table
over, with a casual "hey guys,"
takes a swig, asks what
we're talking about.

You wink, take a big ole
swallow of Marzen,
"You wanna tell him, or should I?"

I clear my throat, smile,
and give the Cliffs Notes of the tenets
of Calvinism, our varying positions
on the validity of the Electoral College,
and how you love the sax but
the cello pulls my heart open.

"Don't forget hip hop versus
modern and why Whitney Houston
is the greatest singer of all time."

"Right, right. Sorry.
Yup, those too."

Eyes wide, slow head shake,
laughs, "Shit, y'all. I was just
gonna say how nice it is that the sun
finally showed up."

I laugh, sip the Maibock, and slip my feet
out of yellow shoes, prop them up
on the opposite chair.
You laugh, lean against
a support beam for the over-
grown pergola.

We three cheers spring, bid
summer to hold off just a bit,
and glory in the light.

Also? I really hate dating

Strangers share a drink—coffee
tea, whisky, hot chocolate—and tell
the same stories from the last time
they met a woman. Stories with no room
for interjection or comment, other than
"how fascinating," "that must've been hard,"
"you poor thing!" "well aren't you brilliant!"

I used to get nervous, sending texts
to friends with outfit options
(not the black pencil skirt,
never the black pencil skirt
on a first or second date).

But then I realized
my perfume was no match
for the stench that had seeped
through three layers of spaghetti-
stained cotton. I should've studied
up on conspiracy theories and Fortnite
instead of making sure my anxiety
acne was well camouflaged.

Now? Now I want to meet a familiar
fella for a beer and have real
conversations about *The Handmaid's Tale*,
Hogwarts, how modern basketball uniforms
look like jammies.

I want the thrill the sound
of his text (tweetie bird, drums, calypso?)
gives my heart before I even read it;
brunch at the terrible tavern
that has bottomless Bloody Marys
and a booth for our (OUR?!?!?!) friends;
him to want to meet my father,
laugh with my mother, tell me
I'm the pretty sister.

I want the tingle that shimmies
all the way up my arm when his
pinkie brushes mine.

Casserole Gatekeeper

I was on my second beer
at my usual place on my usual
day, and he'd just had wings with my father
who is still talking about the french fries.

I told him to prepare, that the casseroles
were coming and not to trust
a woman wearing a trench coat.

I explained that accepting some steaming
dish of creamed soup and fried onions
was an implicit agreement. He needed
a gatekeeper, someone to shoo away
the over-eager bearing lidded Pyrex.

We told the truth, in all the ickiness,
because we are better than polite lies
and false assurances.

I promised to never dress up
reality and to keep the marginally
anything from crossing his threshold.

He laughed, I laughed.
And I reminded him that there are no
rules, no right way for the after.

How I Love

I will bathe in your smile
until my skin glows gold
and drape your laugh
around my neck, a silver locket
disappearing between my breasts.

I'll weave sweaters
from your tears that I might
wear the wool of your pain,
purpled bruises pressed
into your heart since before
my time, a sweating sacrifice
so you may traipse in cotton.

I am porch-sitting with Glennon Doyle,

 drinking tea, swinging in the pumpkin
chair, convinced we are best friends.
I had to go inside to get a pen—
her truth is spilling out
untamed and I'm afraid
to miss a single word, already
decided to go back,
read it again
as soon as I finish
the last page.

It is a prayer, a meditation,
and I feel it echoing in all
my past lives, vibrating back
to when I was a mother, trembling
into the future of goddaughters.
I am a dragon; I am a polar bear;
I am a cheetah. I want to throw
all the keys to the caged.

Shadow Boxer

There is a spot the size of a lemon
tucked beneath my left shoulder blade
that aches with a new pain
and I'm proud.

I've taken up boxing,
a balance to a decades long
yoga practice, aggression released
to make room for zen.

I've learned to jab, cross,
uppercut, and hook. I can bob
and weave, but I'm no butterfly—
sweat dripping off my nose, running
in rivers between my breasts.

When the countdown dings, the combination
of punches and shuffles complete, I fold
at the waist, slick palms resting
on slicker knees, my breath
an inconsistent staccato.

Tomorrow I will creak out
of my bed and beat back
stagnation, again.

Olly Olly Oxen Free

Shakespeare was wrong—
I side with cummings.*

I've been labeled Mrs., girl,
lady, bitch, pork-pork, slut,
Dairy Queen, Elsie, Slow Rowe...
Dad still calls me Buggy.

I am not what you make me,
as if your words could define
an existence that only dances
in this plane—kissing the earth
with moments of clarity and grace.

I have cut off all that is not me—
bleeding out someone else's truth,
leaving only myself—bones, muscles,
ligaments, giggles, whispers, sighs.

These scars on skin (my scars,
my skin) are caesarean
and I claim my name.

*It takes courage to grow up to be who you really are. - e.e. cummings

Laughing with Lydia

I watch him watch her
maneuver the up down up down
of the platform in the back
corner of our brewery.

The up isn't the problem—
she hoists herself over the lip,
a baby seal finding space
on the iceberg—but the down
makes me hold my breath
and grab his arm.

And all he does is cock
his right eyebrow, slip his hand
under her belly, and ease
her to the floor.
Lydia giggles, turns
and goes right back up.
And down and up and
down again.

Until she doesn't need her daddy's
hand to hold her up
anymore. "She's got it,
she's learned a new thing."

He scoops her up, her squeals
a rollercoaster of joy, make him
laugh, me laugh, and I see it.

A delight so pure that love
seems too small a word bubbling
from deep inside and out into
the world passes from father
to daughter and back again.

Grief

Some wrap grief
around their shoulders
tucked in tight,
clasped against
their heart—
fists balled, knuckles
white against
the grey blanket.

Grief lives in my body,
swelling ankles,
causing uterus
to push against
dermis, warping
the shape of belly.
My hip joints ache
like after a flu that
refuses to leave.

I'm not just sad,
I'm mourning, exhausted,
disappointed, angry.
Lonely.

I've collected blankets
from anyone weeping
and pile them on—
quilts of tears and screams
settle over my bloat

as I nestle into the couch
corner and try to remember
to eat.

Scurvy

I have made my bed of disappointments,
a weighted blanket so familiar
it is almost comfortable.

I am afraid
of taking up space
in a world that does not
want me to breathe
deep or speak much beyond
"I've got it, I understand, don't
worry about me, how can I
help?"

I hold hands and broken
hearts and pretend blisters
on my palm aren't oozing, apologizing
if my gunk gets in their creases, praying
my own heart scars don't open
while I listen to tales of betrayal
and how someone let someone else
down.

Tonight I am alone, with my cat,
drinking pinot grigio, never chardonnay,
and tomorrow I will rally
to encourage and heal wounds
and maybe find peroxide
for my own.

Fall into Fantasy

At 8:32 on a Saturday morning
it is still 57 degrees
in my house (MY house)
and my Hobbit slippers
are calling to me from beside
my down comforted bed.

Fleece leggings and Dad's college sweater,
now with thumb holes, and I set off
to the kitchen to put the kettle on.
This morning calls for Smoke
from Harney and Sons with a dollop,
or two, of Carolina Cream.

I fold into the tufted tweed couch
that reminds Mom of Nana.
The fuzzy ombre orange blanket
is a cat nest, so I grab the throw
from off the navy velvet chair
and snuggle in deeper.

A mashed button on the remote
brings my fake fire to life and I try
not to giggle at the startled Minerva
who has drool on her whiskers.

I curl the roughhewn mug against
my breastbone, warmth reddening
my chest, and I gaze out past my porch
into the turning maple tree, the novel
forgotten for a long moment.

And I am happy.

"We don't do math,"

she reminds me, again,
when I tell the bartender
at Single Brothers we've been
friends longer than we haven't.

I reminisce over her stripper hair,
blonde curls too blonde, big bangs too big,
and she teases my Gap dancer
ensemble: tucked in tee and belted khakis.

She photographed my wedding,
the beginning of an end,
caught secret smiles, blushes,
believed in my hopefulness.

I cried with her over the phone
when she learned little
baby sunshine head would be
her only child.

She held me on Main Hall's
back porch at two in the morning
when I told her my uterus
was broken so I must be, too.

This woman who told me,
"honey come home"
when I had to flee my house
or be buried in it,

is tattooed on my skin, deeper—
on my very bones.

On Missing Nana

Nana died twenty-three years ago next month,
and today I realized that the ache
has grown up with me.

It isn't enough to know she'd be proud
of me and this world I've built from a broken
heart, buoyed by her blood.

I want to show her my house, packed
to the rafters with stories, rooted
by her credenza.

She would hug the necks of my people, telling
tales of Christmas candlelights
and twirly Polly Flenders dresses.

Jurassic Park still elicits giggles
when the T-Rex chases the Jeep,
I can hear her "Oh! Oh!"

And smell the sour balls
stuck in the armrest of the grey Mercury
on our way to deliver Meals on Wheels.

Really, I wish I could hold her
hand, rest my cheek on her shoulder,
and breath in her Desert Flower perfume.

Grief Like a Mustard Seed

I carry it with me, always,
carved into the underside
of my sternum, a secret tattoo
that never heals against the thwap
thawpping of my heart.

Sometimes the ink bleeds
into my dreams and his face
like some horror movie villain
peeks in all the windows and the cops
only laugh at my cries for help.

But sometimes I'm the face
on the other side of the glass
peeping at the picture-perfect
family of daughters around
the dining room table.

The guru said we all carry a grief
or loss or sadness or joy-thief
somewhere in our bodies, small
enough to go unnoticed by passersby
or friends. Ignoring causes rot and decay
to break-off into the bloodstream where
it becomes a part of every part of me.

So instead I water the seed
in faith that it will grow
a greater love
than grief.

That tree will be beautiful.

Nice Things

There's no good place to bathe
the 64lb lapdog so I pay
with a coupon and some editing
cash to get him groomed by Betty
with the snuff-stained smock
at PetSmart.

I tell him he's the reason
we can't have nice things
as I re-tuck the couch cover
and roll my eyes at the slightly browner
rag rug in the living room.

What I don't tell him—

this bundle of drama-filled
sighs and harrumphs who cannot
tolerate a moped driving by
and has created a red clay
path along the privacy fence
built to pacify the gentlemen
next door who feared
for their aged chihuahua,

whose muscles are a marriage
of a powerlifter and ballerina
when he bounds off the porch
to catch a butterfly,

holds the heads of the feral kittens
soft in his mouth and cries
to play with them when they
scratch at the glass door,

shoves his heavy head
under my arm during
morning meditation and circles
the rug by my bed three
times before doughnutting
for sleep—

he, he is the nice thing.

For Melissa and Jimmy on the Occasion of Their Leveling Up

I believe in love born out of silly conversations
in the glow of porch lights listening to Daughter;

unabashed dancing in a jellybean
car after lying in a field
to watch the stars whisper secrets;

framily game night that dissolves
into epithets and giggles when grownups compete;

cats in strollers for neighborhood walks
where lookers-on peek through gauzy curtains
and try to read the tattoos.

I believe that peace comes from holding hands
in the present, knowing the past, and gazing into the future.

Auld Lang Syne

As the year goes dark,
I set my gratitude on fire.
Every evening of every day
I take a moment, a minute,
to write thank you—

for my parents, the best house-hunters
        a grownup girl could want,
for my cat who no longer lives
        exclusively under my bed,
for roasted Brussels sprouts and
        bacon ends.

I fold each square,
creasing the edges, and drop
them in a box that used
to hold terrible wine.

On the last night,
I sit, with good wine,
and read. I read each
dated note that builds
a story of my place
in this rotation.

When every glad is accounted
and remembered, out comes

the metal bowl, and I go
out back bundled in wool
and memories.

I set fire to each
grateful and watch
as the embers of the good
of the year flit to help
light the darkness.

Raindrops on Rowes-es

I've decided the perfect time
for strolls is 12:17 a.m. in the gleam
of Narnia lamps, too bright
but for the downpour that makes
the walk to my car almost a swim.

My blue rain boots nearly glow
as they squish in puddles, sand
teasing the soles, sucking
the rubber with lewd exclamations
upon release.

I laugh, face to the heavens, arms
wide, the birds of my scarf
drowning, clinging to my shirt,
my neck, and I lose
balance when my shoe succumbs
to the embrace of the mud.

He grabs my arm, keeping me
from kissing concrete.

Steady on
to the car and the rain slows.
We're already soaked through
so he leans against my trunk and asks me
where did I come from
and I say Morganton, North Carolina.

He laughs, shakes his head,
and the hours dissolve,
powdered sugar on my tongue.

Time Zones

You are so far away
that the moment
the tide carries you
one direction or the other
you are on your way
back to me.

When I miss you the most
I make something strong
in the Hedwig mug
and sleep in the heathered
orange sweatshirt I stole
years before I knew how much
comfort it can bring. I told you
it felt like being wrapped in
an afghan and I didn't care that it
made me look like I'd had the flu
for ten days. You said
I was lovely in it, stole it back,
wore it, and snuck it in my closet.

Last night I missed you so much
that no tea or sweatshirt could
ease the ache that had seeped
below my skin so that even my
veins felt your absence.

Today you said you'd been gone
for most of the year, and I said

I know. But what I wanted to say
was that the typhoons and pirates
are causing grey hairs
and my worry lines map
my forehead and the sparkle you
said you could see in my eyes
from yesterday's selfie
were the tears that waited five
more minutes to fall.

Spotter

"No, no, Daddy. No,"
declares the new two-
year old, complete
with wagging pointer
finger, after he helps
her into her chair
for dinner. "Okay, baby,"
and she crawls back
down just to climb back
up, standing centered
in her world, secured by her
spotter.

She has no concept of safe
because he is always
up front or in the back-
ground when she takes
off at a dead run
across the field
secured five generations
back. The swing
in the old oak, hung
just for her, cradles the next
adventure.

Even after a tumble
in the yellow and red
plastic coupe, there is no
fear. Just an "I ok.

Halp," knowing he'll
set the world right
again.

She does not know
yet, that bigger hurts
are coming and he
cannot stop them. But
he will kiss every bruise
and every heartache
because he is her
daddy.

Love notes to the felon

are scattered in the ditch
in front of my house.
They are folded under
drying leaves, forgotten Christmas
tree sprigs, and puppy poop
I've thrown over the fence.

These declarations of devotion
in running purple and 80s
pink make me pause, pick up,
and read. This isn't the first
time I've eavesdropped
on the beats of some other
woman's heart. She said before
that he was cruel because he
knew she was off her meds
and couldn't take the flip-
flopping of his attentions. But
she loved him anyway.

I don't feel guilty, this time,
as I read through the ways
she promises herself,
only sad. I know
what it is to be passed
over, to be forgotten, to be
thrown away like the piles
of airplane bottle Fireball
and discarded oxygen tubing.

He's moved on, evicted
from the tumbling down
trailers, and I wonder if she
knows he's gone, really gone,
this time leaving her faded
and torn in a stranger's ditch.

Harvesting Figs While the Puppy Frolics

I'm pretending autumn
this morning even though
I'm watching the dew evaporate
and the mosquitos won't stop
sucking at my toes.

Neville is three months
today and is chasing yellow
jackets and slurping the runoff
from my HVAC unit.

The fruit from this one
tree that I thought dead
is my favorite color
of lipstick and I wish
each bite could dye my lips.

The wooden bowl Mom gave
me years ago when I lived
in the house that was not
mine, is starting to get full
and my fingers are sticky.

I round up the beast
who bounds up the steps
still tripping a bit over
the top one, and we go
inside so I can kiss
his vicious face, thankful

he failed to catch any
insects, wash my hands,
and head off in the heat.

Acknowledgements

My parents are the most ridiculously supportive people and I am forever indebted to them for all things. Not the least of which are Dad's willingness to go toe to toe for the right word and Mom's teary smile and nod and need to leave the room after I read to her.

The Write Minds is an insanely talented group of writers at all stages that make me better with each and every meeting. Thank you all, especially John and James and Katrina.

This book wouldn't have been possible without the sister-friends who shore me up in my darkest days and force me into the sunlight, and sometimes just let me be quiet in their presence. I'm looking at you Alexa, Amie, Christine, Holly, and Mis.

Thank you to Swamp Rabbit Brewery for hosting me either out back or holed up at a table somewhere with countless edits and revisions and first drafts. They kept the beer (Maiboc and Marzen specifically) flowing and the bar flys far away.

And Roger and Mike, the best aunties anybody could ever wish for. You were both right, he is the best.

I'd also like to thank Summer and everyone at Unsolicited Press. They have been a dream to work with and Katie is a genius with covers. Thank you thank you.

Headshot courtesy of Keith Schrecengost of dv8 photography.

About the Author

Rowe Carenen is a graduate of Salem College and the University of Southern Mississippi. When asked, she'd say that poetry has been her passion ever since she realized that words could convey more than just the facts. Her poems have appeared in various literary journals and magazines, including *The Revenant Culture, GERM, Terrible Orange Review*, the *Running with Water* anthology, and her first collection, *In the Meantime*, was published by Neverland Publishing in 2014. She lives in Greenville, South Carolina, with her cat Minerva Jane and dog Neville Jameson.

About the Press

Unsolicited Press is rebellious much like the city it calls home: Portland, Oregon. Founded in 2012, the press supports emerging and award-winning writers by publishing a variety of literary and experimental books of poetry, creative nonfiction, fiction, and everything in between.

Learn more at unsolicitedpress.com.

Find us on twitter and Instagram: @unsolicited

9 781956 692129